First World War
and Army of Occupation
War Diary
France, Belgium and Germany

59 DIVISION
178 Infantry Brigade
Sherwood Foresters
(Nottinghamshire and Derbyshire Regiment)
1/7th Battalion
1 February 1918 - 22 August 1918

WO95/3025/4

The Naval & Military Press Ltd
www.nmarchive.com
Published in association with The National Archives

Published by

The Naval & Military Press Ltd

Unit 10 Ridgewood Industrial Park,

Uckfield, East Sussex,

TN22 5QE England

Tel: +44 (0) 1825 749494

www.naval-military-press.com

www.nmarchive.com

This diary has been reprinted in facsimile from the original. Any imperfections are inevitably reproduced and the quality may fall short of modern type and cartographic standards.

© **Crown Copyright**
Images reproduced by permission of The National Archives, London, England, 2015.

Contents

Document type	Place/Title	Date From	Date To
Heading	WO 3025 59 Div 178 Bde 1/7 BN Sherwood Foresters 1918 Feb-1918 July		
Heading	59 Division 178 Bde 1/7 BN Sherwood Foresters 1918 Feb-1918 July		
War Diary	Gouy En Ternois	01/02/1918	08/02/1918
War Diary	Labret	09/02/1918	09/02/1918
War Diary	Mercatel	11/02/1918	11/02/1918
War Diary	Mory	12/02/1918	17/02/1918
War Diary	Bullecourt Right Sub Sector Right Brigade Section	18/02/1918	28/02/1918
Miscellaneous	Appendix A		
Operation(al) Order(s)	7th (Robin Hood) Battalion The Sherwood Foresters Order No. 103	08/02/1918	08/02/1918
Operation(al) Order(s)	7th (Robin Hood) Battalion The Sherwood Foresters Order No. 104	10/02/1918	10/02/1918
Operation(al) Order(s)	7th (Robin Hood) Battalion The Sherwood Foresters Order No. 105	16/02/1918	16/02/1918
Operation(al) Order(s)	Operation Order No. 106 by Lieut Col W.S.N. Toller D.S.O. Commanding The Robin Hoods	22/02/1918	22/02/1918
Operation(al) Order(s)	Operation Order No 107 by Lieut Col W.S.N. Toller D.S.O. Commanding The Robin Hoods	23/02/1918	23/02/1918
Miscellaneous	Patrol Report		
Miscellaneous	Defence Scheme	27/02/1918	27/02/1918
Miscellaneous	Sheet 2		
Miscellaneous	Sheet 3		
Map	Fontaine Trench Map		
Heading	7th Battalion Sherwood Foresters (robin Hood Battalion) March 1918		
War Diary	Ecoust Left Sector	01/03/1918	01/03/1918
War Diary	Brigade Support	02/03/1918	02/03/1918
War Diary	Mory Labeaye Camp (B22a.9.5)	03/03/1918	10/03/1918
War Diary	Brigade Support (C90.9.4.)	11/03/1918	16/03/1918
War Diary	Noreuil Sector HQ (C11c.65.98)	17/03/1918	22/03/1918
War Diary	3rd Defence Line B23b.3.6.	22/03/1918	26/03/1918
War Diary	Bavincourt	26/03/1918	29/03/1918
Miscellaneous	Appendix A 176th Inf. Bde.		
Heading	179th Brigade 59th Division 1/7 Battalion Notts & Derby Regiment April 1918		
War Diary	Proven	01/04/1918	03/04/1918
War Diary	Winnizeele	04/04/1918	04/04/1918
War Diary	Brandhoek	10/04/1918	10/04/1918
War Diary	Kemmel	12/04/1918	12/04/1918
War Diary	Neuveeglise	13/04/1918	13/04/1918
War Diary	Wulverghem	14/04/1918	14/04/1918
War Diary	Kemmel	15/04/1918	19/04/1918
War Diary	Brandhoek	20/04/1918	20/04/1918
War Diary	Houtkerque	21/04/1918	23/04/1918
War Diary	Proven	26/04/1918	28/04/1918
War Diary	Houtkerque	29/04/1918	29/04/1918
Heading	30th Division 21st Infy Bde 7th Bn Sherwood For May 1918 7th Sherwood		

Heading	War Diary Of The 7th Sherwood Foresters For The Month Of May 1918		
War Diary	Houtkerque	01/05/1918	02/05/1918
War Diary	Watou Area K 17a 2.8	03/05/1918	05/05/1918
War Diary	St Omer	06/05/1918	08/05/1918
War Diary	Blessy	09/05/1918	09/05/1918
War Diary	Bours	10/05/1918	30/05/1918
War Diary	Caumont	01/06/1918	04/06/1918
War Diary	Frucourt	05/06/1918	11/06/1918
War Diary	Monchaux	12/06/1918	15/06/1918
War Diary	Monchy-Sur-Eu	15/06/1918	20/06/1918
War Diary	Pierregot	21/06/1918	22/06/1918
War Diary	Contay	23/06/1918	24/06/1918
War Diary	Pierregot	25/06/1918	26/06/1918
War Diary	St Leger-Le-Domart	27/06/1918	27/06/1918
War Diary	Villers-Sous-Ailly	28/06/1918	30/06/1918
Miscellaneous	Appendix A		
Heading	War Diary Of 7th (Robin Hood) Bn The Sherwood Foresters. From 1/7/18 To 31/7/18 Volume 42		
War Diary	Villers-Sous-Ailly (Lens 11, A6)	01/07/1918	31/07/1918
War Diary	Abancourt	31/07/1918	22/08/1918
Miscellaneous	Appendix A		
Miscellaneous	Appendix B		

WO3025

59 Div 178 Bde

1/7 Bn STERWOOD FORESTERS

1918 Feb — 1918 July

59 DIVISION
17 BDE

1/7 BN SHERWOOD FORESTERS

1918 FEB - 1918 JULY

From 46 DIV, 139 BDE

To 39 DIV Troops

ABSORBED 2/7 BN

WAR DIARY
or
INTELLIGENCE SUMMARY.

(Erase heading not required.)

Army Form C. 2118.

Instructions regarding War Diaries and Intelligence Summaries are contained in F. S. Regs., Part II. and the Staff Manual respectively. Title pages will be prepared in manuscript.

Place	Date	Hour	Summary of Events and Information	Remarks and references to Appendices

Army Form C. 2118.

WAR DIARY
or
INTELLIGENCE SUMMARY.
(Erase heading not required.)

Instructions regarding War Diaries and Intelligence Summaries are contained in F. S. Regs., Part II. and the Staff Manual respectively. Title pages will be prepared in manuscript.

Place	Date	Hour	Summary of Events and Information	Remarks and references to Appendices
	11		The Battalion marched out at 2pm to a Camp near MORY, the ENGINEERS in the areas. Everyone did not an opportunity to use this Camp was about 2½ miles behind the line and the Battalion in Reserve. Between the 9th and 5th Brigade further supplies the NW of BULLECOURT to take Stores Ammunition to the 140th Division in the BULLECOURT sector.	See Appendix D
MORY	12		Training. All Companies Carried out a program of training from 9ab. 2m. Special attention was paid to rapid firing.	
			Leave. 2/Lieut J.L. Hoy proceeded to England on leave.	
			Strength. 2/Lieut F. Batt Reynolds from Hospital and promoted to Quarter Master for duty. Major of Manson proceeded from the 59th Reinforcement Depot AB to take over the duties of Quarter Master of Bn HGQR.	
	13		Nil. Nothing further from the 2 Coys went up the line by motor lorries during the night.	

A5834 Wt. W4973/M687 750,000 8/16 D.D. & L. Ltd. Forms/C.2118/13

Army Form C. 2118.

WAR DIARY
or
INTELLIGENCE SUMMARY.
(Erase heading not required.)

4 February 1918

Instructions regarding War Diaries and Intelligence Summaries are contained in F. S. Regs., Part II. and the Staff Manual respectively. Title pages will be prepared in manuscript.

Place	Date	Hour	Summary of Events and Information	Remarks and references to Appendices
NOEUX	16		Training. A/morning. Training in Coast and strong pts. morning.	
			Lunch. Lieut Col NICKSON lunched on boars to confer with Major T.S WARREN on a look	
			Over Command of Battalion Capt BEECH being 2nd in Command	
			Paid. B. & C.Coy.2 in defensibility. B. defensible to...	
			Enemy planes. Ten Enemy planes flew over NOEUX by our aeros.	
			Operation.	
			Reconnaissance. During the 6 Sept. Bn. Battalion in Divisional reserve a party of officers and nco reconnoitred the Brigade sector Funnel Trench Sap.	
			Parade. The Battalion attended Divine Service to hear MOST. CHE. G. Binns MoY Bushman	
		17	In relief of the 1st Bn. of R.Y. Lancers.	
			Observation party. An advance party under 2Lieut HUDSON went up at 3 p.m. to take over	
			----Tres. a RAILWAY RESERVE to GQHQ	
			Relief. The Battalion relieved the 1st Special Yeomanry in the Right Sub sector. The	New Appdix B and Appx D
			relief was carried out without incident.	
			On our left the 3/6 (Reserve) Yorkshire on our right the 1/7th Argylls. A & B Coys in	
			the Rights sector, C & D Coys on the right, D on my right. E my Appdx E & 4/6 Argylls.	
			1/16 Defence Scheme will be found on Appendix E	

A 5834 Wt W4973/M687 750,000 8/16 D. D. & L. Ltd. Forms/C.2118/13

Army Form C. 2118.

WAR DIARY
or
INTELLIGENCE SUMMARY

(Erase heading not required.)

February 1918

Place	Date	Hour	Summary of Events and Information	Remarks and references to Appendices
BULLECOURT Aux Rietz By Right Sector	18		Rear: 2nd Lieut MARSHALL proceeded to Transport Lines for Course. Captain J. Channing on the 20th.	
			Patrol: A party of 9 O.R.'s and 6 I.R. left lines at 11.50 pm night of 18/19. Reconnoitred TRIDENT ALLEY. They lost direction in foggy and met party thinking to be the Scouting party of D. 2½ R. When they came up again in Enemy Party of about twenty strong, they attempted to entice our party into their trench Their attempt failed. Their Officer (PROM) at a point in FAG TRENCH was killed by our men whose Field was uncut.	
			Enemy Action: Quiet previous to night.	
	19		Strength: Lieut A. TAYLER D.S.O arrived at 4.30 pm from leave in England and took over Duties as Adjutant of S. Papers vice Major J.C. WATSON M.C. of leave per Duty. J gives Command of his Tin Jobs	
			Patrols: Two patrols went out as follows:— (a) Reg Coy, two officers Lieut W PATMORE and 7 O.R.'s enemy sketch new enemy trench at H.21.E (Central, my scheme). They left our front at 10.15 pm and forced to return as the enemy trench previously occupied as a trench by two R.I. Reg This Coy Patrols a strong M.G. encountered doing excellent shooting form the occupied a line losing party to any trench with caused hit and got out in times. He paint intention knowing party or avoided enemy posts prevented any further...	

Army Form C. 2118.

WAR DIARY
or
INTELLIGENCE SUMMARY.
(Erase heading not required.)

Month: February 1918

Place	Date	Hour	Summary of Events and Information	Remarks and references to Appendices
BULLECOURT Right Subsector	19		Sport: Lieut R.W. HOYLE proceeded from III Corps Infantry School to HUMBERCOURT. Patrols Cont'd)	
			(2) Under 2/Lieut C.L. JONES to reconnoitre NEPTUNE TRENCH and report on its condition. They found the trench in parts but many holes being along and damaged. Our wire was intact in most places. No enemy were seen or heard.	See Appendix C
			Enemy Artillery: An easy evening & the 20th. Afterwards our fire on Bn. Rear H.Q. front but otherwise O.K. night was quiet.	
	20		Movement: Our observers saw a great deal of movement notably along CORSE TRENCH and Sunken Rd near U.17 (Central). The enemy seems to be working hard on his trenches.	
			Patrols: On night 20/21 patrols went out as under:-	
			(1) Under 2/Lieut W.F. SPENCER with 1 OR to reconnoitre new German trench at U.21.6.30.60 and a road to ultimately leading to posts. They left our line at 1.15am and returned at 3.30am having made a successful reconnaissance. The leader reported that he considered it easy to possible to carry out a raid. Wire to right flank.	See Officers Coy
			(2) Under 2/Lieut D.J. NUNNICOTT N.C.O. to report on the entrance to Sunken Rd at U.20.a.32. They carried out a successful reconnaissance without being fired on by the enemy.	See Officers from 2

Army Form C. 2118.

WAR DIARY
or
INTELLIGENCE SUMMARY.
(*Erase heading not required.*)

Month: February 1918

Instructions regarding War Diaries and Intelligence Summaries are contained in F. S. Regs., Part II. and the Staff Manual respectively. Title pages will be prepared in manuscript.

Place	Date	Hour	Summary of Events and Information	Remarks and references to Appendices
PUISIEUX Left Subsector	21		**Patrols** Night 20/21st	
			(a) Under Lieut F H CLARK to reconnoitre VULCAN Pit Bn and VULCAN TRENCH - to report to what extent they carried out the reconnaissance without interference from the enemy. Putting in evidence of recent offensive preparations on the part of the enemy in the shape of small fire bays and bomb hoards lying about.	
			(b) Under 2nd Lieut L.A.L. BROWN and 3 O.R. to patrol Left Coy front and report on same.	
			(c) A daylight patrol under Lieut F H CLARK and 1 N.C.O. to enquire information gained in previous night's patrols of SUNKEN Rd in N.M.C. They entered Bn ... NEPTUNE TRENCH over Robbins Capt Rd. Returning to HUNT'S ... any out getting a good view of the SUNKEN Rd and the Valley. They were not interfered with by the Enemy in any way.	For Offensive D
	23		**Patrols** A day light patrol on Orange out by Lieut. D.J. WINNICOTT M.C. and 2 O.R. (Cpl. MIDDLETON Pte. KENTON) of C Coy attempted VULCAN TRENCH getting up as far as N.15.C.30.95 where they were seen and fired on by a sentry, presumably from TRIDENT.	
			Course 2nd Lieut. L.A. STAMS proceeded to a Course at VI Corps Infantry School	
			Leave Capt. C.W. GOOD proceeded to England - 6 months' home duty.	
			Inter Company Relief took place on night 23/24.	

Sheet 2. February 1918

Army Form C. 2118.

WAR DIARY
or
INTELLIGENCE SUMMARY
(Erase heading not required.)

Instructions regarding War Diaries and Intelligence Summaries are contained in F.S. Regs., Part II. and the Staff Manual respectively. Title pages will be prepared in manuscript.

Place	Date	Hour	Summary of Events and Information	Remarks and references to Appendices
BULLECOURT Right Sub Sector	23		Patrols (a) Under 2nd Lieut C. L. Jones (A Co.) and 8 O.R. to reconnoitre stations No mans land and observe enemy movements in the leafy trees. Also to report present class of enemy wire. This two carried out schemes 2 and 3 and S.T.G. on. No enemy being seen or heard. (Unsigned)	See Appendices C and D
			(b) A strong fighting patrol consisting of 2nd Lieut N.E. SPOTTERS also 28 OR - 3 parties to move At enemy front trench in U.21.b on. To obtain identification. They found the trench unoccupied leaving here about occupied out by our Artillery, to be the Wednesday the night.	
			Enemy Artillery was more active than hitherto. Railway RESERVE was shelled by a 5.9 near R.21.9.4.M. LANE during the afternoon.	
			Patrols under 2nd Lieut J.W. WILSON and 10 O.R. to reconnoitre NUBIAN ALLEY from U.14.a.98.07 to U.15.c.89.90 and SANDAN to U.15.c.8. the enemy patrol in strength at (Army U.21.a.6.Y. but disappeared before contact to picket me. from 12 midnight to 2 am.	
	24		Operations Enemy in our left sub sector during night of 23/24 but enemy also was driven off before reaching our trenches by 4 of our Artillery who responded to an S.O.S. call.	

Army Form C. 2118.

Aprl 9 April 1918

WAR DIARY
or
INTELLIGENCE SUMMARY.

(Erase heading not required.)

Instructions regarding War Diaries and Intelligence Summaries are contained in F. S. Regs., Part II. and the Staff Manual respectively. Title pages will be prepared in manuscript.

Place	Date	Hour	Summary of Events and Information	Remarks and references to Appendices
BULLECOURT	1/5	Patrol	A patrol went out under Lieut V.E. HODSON with 2 O.R. to investigate T24.C.5.0.5 and if unsuccessful to push onto DOG TRENCH and report on that. They got on line at N.85 and on reaching the Trench they found that the enemy was holding posts from DOG TRENCH to just in front of the enemy wire. They found that the enemy had improved the Trench the was plainly audible. Our patrol fired on his listening post. They returned to M.S. Post at 4.5 am over and as it was too light to present further.	
	16	About	An enemy plane was brought down by A.A. Guns at 4.35 am and crashed near the FACTORY, BULLECOURT.	See Appendices
	16	Patrols	A daylight patrol consisting of Capt A.L.M. DICKENS M.C., Sgt WATSON and Sgt BLOOD, J. Dcy, went out at 9.30 am into the following speak on rear. (1) To ascertain if the enemy kept a post in VULCAN ALLEY (2) To report on enemy movements between U.10.90.95 and U.15.20.05 (3) To find out if CRUMP ALLEY is connected to VULCAN ALLEY and cross to the SUNKEN Rd between U.15.15.85 and U.15.80.65. At 5 post nightly tops Sgt HARRISON and Sgt REAVILL J. Dcy went out to reconnoitre These lived and fired is manned by the Enemy	C

Army Form C. 2118.

WAR DIARY
or
INTELLIGENCE SUMMARY.
(Erase heading not required.)

Place	Date	Hour	Summary of Events and Information	Remarks and references to Appendices
BULLECOURT Right Sub sector	Feb 10 1918		Patrols (Cont.)	
	26		2nd Lieut WILLIAMSON (D Coy) took out a fighting patrol 1 "B" OR and a L.G. and lay in road for the Enemy. The Enemy was actively patrolling our front in NEPTUNE TRENCH. They came up again and our Men a party entered at pm 30.10 40, but were unable to find any Casualties as carrying the ground afterward.	
			At 9.15 am Lieut 6/62, 2nd Lieut HUDSON went out with 9 OR on our Right to gain information about D.O.1 TRENCH and came across an Enemy working party and also a Strong Point. An Enemy M.G. opened on our patrol next to Enemy Patrol licence off without pursuit.	
			Leave. Major J.E. WARREN M.C. proceeded to England on leave.	
			Cmdng. 2nd Lieut N.F. SPENCER proceeded to II Army Musketry Camp WAR COY.	
	27		Patrols 2nd Lieut HUDSON took out a fighting patrol 9.10 OR with a L.G. & NEPTUNE TRENCH. The Boche was seen but When Patrol got near no could only hit at and subsequently the Patrol was got home. Huns also threw some Cigs. All Enemy had not some of the own offensive moths spot.	

A5834. Wt. W4973/M687. 750,000. 8/16. D. D. & L. Ltd. Forms/C.2118/13

WAR DIARY
INTELLIGENCE SUMMARY

February 1918

Place	Date	Hour	Summary of Events and Information	Remarks and references to Appendices
Bullecourt (Left Subsector)	27	(Cont)	At 6.20 p.m. 2/Lieut T. Williamson took out 1 O.R. and 1 L.G. to raid an enemy patrol near NEPTUNE TRENCH. They were seen about 30 yds from our front line and fired on by rifle during approach from NEPTUNE TRENCH. One L.G. was in Neptune. The Patrol withdrew and an enemy M.G. traversed the line from somewhere on the left. The party became involved and dispersed to find a position and put the enemy into confusion.	
	29		Patrol A patrol consisting of 2 Officers and 10 O.R. under Capt A.L.M. DICKENS M.C went out to reconnoitre NEPTUNE and to ascertain if the enemy held it at night but a left M.G. and fire fell in trail for any enemy patrols between U.21.a.8.50 and U.21.a.30.55	Appendix C

M.I.R. Toller Lt. Col.
7th (Robin Hood) Battn.
(SHERWOOD FORESTERS,
NOTTS. & DERBY REGT.)

APPENDIX 'A'.

	Officers.	O. Ranks.
Total Strength of Battalion January 31. 18.	46.	993.

Total Fighting strength.	35.	809.		
On Command.				
Brigade Employ.	1.	21.		
Div. "		8.		
T.M. Battery.		7.		
M.G. Coy.		4.		
Leave.	4.	46.		
Hospital.		44.		
Courses.	5.	43.		
Depot Battalion.	1.	11		
	46.	993.	46.	993.

Total Strength February 1st. 1918.			46.	993.
Increase.				
Reinforcements.	3.	68.		
Rejoined.	1.	11.	4.	79.
			50.	1072.
Decrease.				
Evacuated.		28.		
Trans. to M.G. Coy.		4.		32.
			50.	1040.

Total Strength of Battn. Feb. 28th. 1918.			50.	1040.
Total Fighting Strength.	36.	834.		
On Command.				
Brigade Employ.	1.	25.		
Div. "	1.	30.		
T.M. Battery.		9.		
Leave.	4.	25.		
Hospital.		26.		
Courses.	7.	42.		
Depot Battalion.	1.	34.		
No. 2 Coy. A.T.C.		2.		
170 Tunlg. Coy. R.E.		13.		
	50.	1040.	50.	1040.

SECRET.   Copy. No.
              7th (Robin Hood) Battalion. The Sherwood Foresters.
                          ORDER No. 103.

                                         In the Field. Feb. 8th. 1918.

Ref. Maps:-   Sheet 51c 1/40.000
               Sheet 51b 1/40.000

(1).   The Battalion will proceed by march route to YORK CAMP to-morrow

(2).   The Battalion will parade in full marching order in fours
        facing N.E. with head of column on Road Junction at V.4.d.1.4.
        ready to move off at 11.10 a.m.

(3).   Order of march.
                    Battalion Headquarters, Bugle Band, "D", "B",
        "A", "C", Coy's. Medical Officer and Personnel, Transport.

(4).   Starting Point.
                    The starting point is cross roads at Q.23.d.9.5.
        and it will be passed at 1. 5 p.m.

(5).   Route.
                    BRETENCOURT - BLAIRVILLE - FICHEUX - YORK CAMP.

(6).   Intervals of 200 yards will be maintained between companies
        before moving off and during the march.

(7).   Transport.
                    1st. Line Transport and Baggage Wagons will
        march 200 yards in rear of "C" Coy. On arrival Transport will
        be parked at M.16.d.

(8).   March Discipline.
                    Officers Commanding Companies will be held
        responsible that the strictest march discipline is maintained.
        No man will be allowed to fall out without the permission of an
        Officer in writing.

(9).   Administrative Instructions will be issued later.

(10).   Reports to head of Column.

(11).   Acknowledge.

                                              F. PRAGNELL.
                                              Capt & Adjt.
                                    7th (Robin Hood) Bn. The Sherwood Foresters.

Issued at 6. 0 p.m. by runner.
Distribution - Normal.

SECRET.   Copy. No. _____
                7th. (ROBIN HOOD) BATTALION. SHERWOOD FORESTERS.
                              ORDER No. 104.

                                                    In the Field. Feb 10th. 18.
        Ref. Maps:- LENS. 1/100.000
                    51b.   1/40.000
                    57c.   1/40.000

(1).   The Battalion will proceed by march route to MORY NORTH CAMP to-morrow.
        The Quartermasters Stores and Transport Lines will be at ARMAGH No.
        2 Camp, S.23.c.5.0.

(2).   The Battalion will parade in mass facing E. on ground on N. side of
        Camp, ready to move off at 2. p.m.
        Markers will report to R.S.M. at 1. 45 p.m.

(3).   Order of march.   Battalion H.Q. "B", Bugle Band, "C", "D", "A", Coy.
        Medical Officer and personnel, Transport.   Transport will proceed
        direct to Lines. (The Bugle Band will not play after leaving
                                                            ERVILLERS.)

(4).   Route.   MERCATEL - ERVILLERS - MORY.

(5).   Intervals of 200 yards will be maintained between Companies during
        the march.

(6).   Transport.   1st. Line Transport and Baggage Wagons will march
        200 yards in rear of "A" Coy.

(7).   March Discipline.   Officers commanding Coy's will be held
                             responsible that the strictest march discipline is
        maintained. No man will be allowed to fall out without the permiss-
        ion of an Officer in writing.

(8).   Reports to head of Column.

(9).   Acknowledge.

                                                    F. PRAGNELL.
                                                    Capt & Adjt.
                                    7th(Robin Hood)Bn. The Sherwood Foresters.

Issued at 7. 30 p.m. by runner.
Distribution - Normal.

SECRET.   Copy. No.
                    7th (ROBIN HOOD) BATTALION. THE SHERWOOD FORESTERS.
                                    ORDER No. 105.

                                            In the Field. 16-2-18.
Ref. Map. 51b. S.W.

(1).   The Battn. will relieve the 2/5th Battn. Sherwood Foresters, on the right Subsector on the night of 17/18th.

(2).   Companies will relieve opposite numbers as under:-

7th. Bn.	2/5th. Bn.	Position.
"A" Co.	"A" Co.	Right Front Line.
"B" Co.	"B" Co.	Railway Reserve.
"C" Co.	"C" Co.	Left Front Line.
"D" Co.	"D" Co.	Main Support.

(3).   Companies will parade ready to move off as under:-

"A" Co.	5. 15 p.m.
"C" Co.	5. 30 p.m.
"B" Co.	5. 45 p.m.
"D" Co.	6. 0 p.m.
Battn. H.Q.	6. 15 p.m.

Intervals of 50 yards will be maintained between platoons during the march.

(4).   Guides will be provided as under:-
        1 Guide per Coy. and Battn. H.Q. at Brigade Headquarters.
        1 Guide per post and 1 for remainder of Company at 5th Battn. H.Q. for "A" and "C" Coy's.
        1 Guide per platoon at 5th. Battn. H.Q. for "D" Co.

(5).   ROUTE.

        Brigade H.Q. thence via POST TRACK (B.11.c.5.3.) to CRUX CIRCUS. (where road crosses Railway. in U.25.a.)

(6).   Completion of relief will be reported by wire by code word BADGER.

(7).   Acknowledge.

                                                            F. PRAGNELL.
                                                            Capt & Adjt.
                                              7th(Robin Hood)Battn. The Sherwood Fors.

Issued at.......p.m. by runner.
Distribution - Normal plus 2/5th. S. F.

SECRET
Copy No. _____

OPERATION ORDER No. 106.

BY
LIEUT-COL. W.S.N. TOLLER. D.S.O.
Commanding: The Robin Hoods.
Ref. Map. 51.bS.W. In the Field. 22-2-18.

---

(1). Inter Company reliefs will take place on the night 23/24th. inst as under:-
    Letter "B" Coy. will relieve Letter "A" Coy. in Right Front Line and VALLEY SUPPORT.
    Letter "D" Coy. will relieve Letter "C" Coy. in Left Front Line and VALLEY SUPPORT.

(2). On relief Letters "A" and "C" Coy's will occupy the positions and accomodation vacated by Letters "B" and "D" Coy's respectively.

(3). Reliefs will take place after dusk. All details of relief will be arr -anged between O's/C. Coys. concerned.

(4). ADVANCE PARTIES.
    Letters "B" and "D" Coy's will send small advance parties to take over accomodation, S.A.A. Trench Stores, etc, during daylight.

(5). All Trench and Area Stores, S.A.A., Petrol tins, etc, will be handed over and receipts given - Lewis Guns and magazines (excepting those containing A.P. and Tracer S.A.A.) will not be handed over. Copies of receipts will be sent to Battn. Hd. Qrs. within 24 hours of relief.

(6). Completion of relief will be reported to Battn. Hd. Qrs. by wire by Code Word FOXY.

(7). Acknowledge.

                                          F. PRAGNELL.
                                        Capt & Adjt.
                            7th(Robin Hood. Battalion.
                            The Sherwood Foresters.

Issued at 7. 30 p.m. by runner.

Distribution - Normal.
   Plus Headquarters. 178th Inf. Bde.

SECRET.   Copy No. a

OPERATION ORDER No. 107.

By
LIEUT-COL. W.S.N. TOLLER. D.S.O.
Commanding.   The Robin Hoods.
                                               In the Field. 23-2-18.
Ref. Map. 51.b.s.w.

(1). An offensive patrol, with the object of obtaining identification will be carried out against the enemy T. head trench in U.21.b. on the night 23/24th. Feb, 1918.

(2). The patrol will consist of 1 Officer and 25 other ranks of the Robin Hoods and will be in 3 parties as under:-
   Party "A". Sergt. Harrison and 5,O.Rs.
   "   "B". 2/Lt. Spatcher and 10, O.Rs.
   "   "C". Sergt. Fearn and 10, O.Rs.

(3). Party "A" will take up a position on the parapet of the C.T. at about U.21.b.60.62. and be prepared to cover the rear of Party "B" and engage any of the enemy who attempt to reach the T. head or return to COPSE TRENCH.

Party "B" will move round to the rear of the T. head, enter it on the S.E. side of the C.T. and obtain identification.

Party "C" will take up a position at about U.21.b.50.32. and act as covering party to Parties "A" and "B". They will at once engage any of the enemy who may be seen.

(4). As soon as Party "B" have completed their task the Officer in charge will blow his whistle as a signal to Party "A" to return.
Party "C" will remain in position till Parties "A" and "B" have passed and reported all clear.

(5). The dress of the parties will be as follows:-
Rifle and Bayonet, 5 rds S.A.A. in the magazine, 1 in the chamber, safety catch back, 10 rds in the pocket and 2 Mill's bombs.
Steel helmets, Box-respirator in "ALERT" position.
Equipment will not be worn.

(6). All means of identification will be removed from all ranks, Officer in charge will be responsible that this is done.
Letters, papers, identity discs, etc, will be left behind and each man will carry in his top left hand jacket pocket a slip of paper with Number and Name written on.

(7). Should any casualties occur to any of our men they must be brought back to our lines without fail.

(8). The patrol will leave our lines at 3. a.m.

(9). No M.G. will fire short bursts on COPSE TRENCH from 3. 30 a.m. till 5. 30 a.m.

(10). Acknowledge.

                                               F. PRAGNELL.
                                               Capt & Adjt.
                                    7th(Robin Hood)Bn. The Sherwood Foresters.

Issued at 2 p.m. by runner.
Distribution - Normal.

20/2/17

Patrol Report.

Unit	Strength of Patrol	Objective or Task (Fighting or Reconnaissance &c)	Time & Date	Remarks and Information (Route, Information gained, Action of enemy &c.)
1st Robin Hoods. A Coy.	1 Officer 1 Sgt. 6 men	To reconnoitre near German Trench at U.21.a.95.60.50.60 (approx) & discover if there is any wire in front, if there is a possibility of getting behind with a view to eventually doing a raid	Start. U.21.a.95.25 1.15 a.m. Finish U.21.a.95.25 3.30 a.m.	Patrol left our front line at U.21.a.95.25 & moved (guard in direction of objective). Patrol had proceeded about 200 yds when it saw 4 of the enemy working outside their trench failed altogether. They unfortunately however before that the hostile party would walk into them. Patrol hastened & expected [illegible] to be a [illegible] having U.21.b or recovering the party, with I am walked toward U.21.b flank of Point U.21.b.60.50 from line it could be seen that [illegible] of the enemy had taken up a position behind their own line & were apparently acting as a covering party for a working party in the trench as a sound of wire & sandbags would be heard. Patrol leader & 10 of them proceeded to work round the rear of the post, however encountered another working party (Patrol leader & 10 of them proceeded to work round the rear of [illegible]. Patrol leader encountered another working party so were not engaged. Party then proceeded to reconnoitre the rear of the post, but as I am not prepared so what would be [illegible] shall be [illegible] of the post could it came to communication trench leading back from post to Corpse Trench. It reached the point U.21.b.60.70 (approx). It was now [illegible] exhausted working party of good numbers & any strength. There was encountered [illegible] interference by the enemy. Patrol leader then returned to own support [illegible] on but the hostile covering party. Patrol leader noted [illegible] would be difficult to raid post from the front on account of lightness of the hostile taking post or working party with [illegible] be seen & given warning to garrison in post. He is of opinion however that it would be possible to a raiding party to work round the right flank of the post & attack them rear with a fair chance of surprise. This flank appears to be weak. None did not see any officer to be anyone working it. There were no hostile covering party at work on the post. With the exception of the four which fired at the patrol the work of the front was not known by the enemy.

(Sd.) Norman F. Spalden. 2/Lt. A Coy The Robin Hoods.

Patrol Report.

Night 20/21st Sep.

Patrol				
Unit	Strength of Patrol	Time and date	Objective or Task. (Fighting or Reconnaissance &c.)	Remarks & Information. (Route, information gained, action of enemy &c.)
4th (Robin Hood) Bn. Notts. & Sherwood Foresters	1 Officer (H.A.J. Winncott) 8 O.R.	Night 20/21 12.30 a.m.	To report on the entrance to SUNKEN ROAD at U.21.a.32.91.	The patrol left our front line at about 12 post (U.20.C.73.80.) and proceeded along NEPTUNE TRENCH as far as NEPTUNE PILL BOX (U.21.c.33.67.) where it moved in a northerly direction & reached the road junction at U.21.c.20.80. Here except the ground being churned up by shell fire & no stone wall, but craters full of water. The patrol then went forward & reached to the entrance of the SUNKEN ROAD which was found after some time. It is hardly recognisable & does not become a sunkit a point so reached about U.15.c.50.10. During the time out the patrol saw no signs of the enemy, neither were any WEREY LIGHTS or Machine Guns fired. The patrol having completed its task returned to our line at the point of departure.

(sd) H.A.J. Winncott 2/Lt
O.C. Patrol

Copy:-

Patrol Report.

Unit	Strength of Patrol	Time	Objective or Task (Fighting or reconnaissance &c)	Remarks & Information (Route, information gained, action if enemy &c)
1/8(Robin Hood) Bn The Sherwood Foresters	1 Officer 6 O.R.	10.25 p.m. to 11.45 p.m. 21.2.18	To reconnoitre VULCAN and VULCAN trench.	Left out post (U.20.c.7.8) & proceeded along VULCAN trench with 2 men on each flank. Route difficulty was of ground on the flanks. We found the VULCAN trench to be badly damaged & untenable. VULCAN trench is fairly good & dry & 2 or 3 men could easily get along in daylight. On the northern side of the trench a number of shell holes have been prepared as fire bays, & in route cover there are German bombs & empty VEREY Light Cartridges on the parapet. When about 200 yards beyond the western end of the trench reported our enemy working parties on the ridge to the north. We turned left & went about (150 yards of the ridge but could see no enemy. We recrossed the ground & re & found a dead German. We returned to the trench & followed it about another 100 yards without seeing any enemy. No lights were sent up in this front & returning took place. A winter track was noticed on the northern parapet of VULCAN trench. This left the trench & struck in a N.W. direction across the ridge. The patrol returned along the valley S. of the trench & re-entered our line at point of departure.

(a) D.F. Clark. Lt.
O.C. Patrol.

Ref 23/20 4th Feb 1918

Patrol Report.

| A Coy (Robin Hoods) 7th (Robin Hoods) Sherwood Foresters | 1 Offr. 25 OR | Place 3.25 am 24/2/18 Finish 5.40 am 24/2/18 | To raid enemy T head trench in U.21.b with the object of obtaining information | Patrol left our trenches at 3.30 am and proceeded towards objectives. The blocking party took up its position as arranged, at U.21.b.60.62 (approx). The covering party was left at about U.21.b.50.32. Party B then entered S.E. corner of T head. The trench was found to be empty. It had been greatly knocked about by our Artillery fire, some sandbags having been blown off the parapet onto the floor. The trench was only about 5'6" deep. There were a few apparently fresh footprints in S.E. corner, otherwise no signs of enemy occupation. The trench had evidently been made untenable by our artillery fire. Patrol searched all round vicinity of trench but finding no signs of enemy, returned to our lines.

(Sd) N.F. Spalding 2/Lt |

Copy.

Morning 23.2.18.
REF. FONTAINE 10.000

Patrol Report.

Unit	Strength of Patrol	Time & Date	Objective of Patrol (Fighting or Reconnaissance)	Remarks & Information. (Route, information gained, action of enemy &c.)
Robin Woods	1 Officer (2nd Lt J. Winnick M.C.) 2 O.R. (L/Cpl Mitchelson & Pte Ruston)	8.30 a.m. 23.2.18	To reconnoitre VULCAN TRENCH & ascertain if same is probably held by the enemy.	The patrol left our front line from K.0.12 Point (U.20.c.70.80) & worked its way in a Northerly direction as far as NEPTUNE TRENCH as far as VULCAN PILL BOX (U.21.a.00.70) where it arrived in a Northerly organised shell hole containing new bombs & 4 bandoliers of ammunition laid out on the firestep. There were quite a my. & did not appear to have been there during the recent rain. Also there are new footmarks both in the trench & on the Northern parapet & considering that same was full of their night ago there has been a certain amount of how the patrol deduced that the point shewn all along VULCAN TRENCH as far as U.15.c.30.25. where it became very hostile the point being used by the enemy. After having gained this information the patrol proceeded along VULCAN TRENCH as far as U.15.c.30.25. where it became very hostile the point were evidently seen by the enemy as we were subjected at by an m.m. who certainly knew how & where to shoot. We pushed on the top & were fired at again, presumably from TRIDENT ALLEY about U.15.c.to.10. Ho observance is only officer as it was very difficult to locate exactly the position from which the shots came. The patrol carried at this point for about 15 minutes but no enemy movement was seen & we were able to were fired. No one appeared to be there. On reaching a point about U.15.c.20.20 one of the enemy dead was noticed in a shell hole about 15 yards from the trench. He was examined but no identification was found. He had been dead possibly three weeks, as his flesh & hair were to a certain amount still there. His pockets were full of S.A.A & the patrol deducted that he had been sniped on a raider but had been sniped. At this point the patrol left out of the trench on the western side, & just before reaching VULCAN PILL BOX another enemy dead was found & two books were taken from his pocket. No other identification was found. This man had been dead some considerable time. The patrol then worked its way into VULCAN TRENCH again & came back to our lines to opening at the point of departure. In my opinion daylight patrols on this front ought not to go out. As the enemy is on the alert for such & a target against the form early even though they might be covered by a Rum bry. Also that a certain amount of P.H. helmets should be kept with troops for daylight patrols, as it was difficult to wear in a gas respirator.

(S) J. Winnick Lt. O.C. Patrol.

Copy.   26/27th.

Patrol Report.

Unit	Strength of Patrol	Time & Date	Objective or Task (Fighting or Reconnaissance)	Remarks and Information (Route, information gained, action of enemy &c.)
1/7 (Robin Hood) Bn. Sherwood Foresters.	Three. Capt. A.F.W. Aickman. Sgt. Watson. Sgt. Flood.	26.2.18 Departure. 9.30 a.m. U.20.c.70.80 Return 11.35 a.m. U.20.c.70.80	Reconnaissance Patrol. Task. (1) To ascertain if the enemy held a post in VULCAN ALLEY. (2) If CRUMP ALLEY is connected to VULCAN ALLEY & through to the sunken road between U.15.c.80.65 & U.15.c.55.85 (3) To report on condition of wire, if any, between U.15.c.55.85 and U.15.c.80.05	Patrol left no.13 post at U.20.c.70.80 at 9.30 a.m. getting into VULCAN ALLEY & following the trench up to VULCAN Pill-Box. Sgt. Watson personally examined the Pill Box and on reporting to me that the Pill Box shewed no signs of occupation we proceeded up VULCAN to U.15.c.40.30. After observing the left flank for a short time we saw what appeared to be a trench about 400 yds to our left flank. Patrol got out of VULCAN & walked across towards the supposed trench. Four shots were fired at us by a sniper from the direction of TRIDENT which caused us to take cover in a shell hole. We crawled up to the supposed trench & discovered that it was not a trench, but merely a series of shell holes. Patrol then doubled back to VULCAN & carried on up VULCAN to about U.15.c.70.65 at which point a trench was seen branching to VULCAN which was CRUMP ALLEY. Patrol turned up VULCAN another 20 yds & discovered a trench running from VULCAN ALLEY to CRUMP ALLEY from U.15.c.73.67 to U.15.c.50.80. but it did not run through VULCAN to the sunken road. There was no wire between U.15.c.73.67 to U.15.c.50.80. The trench is apparently a communication trench. Patrol was about to return to our lines when a Boche sentry carrying a steel helmet which had been placed recently was seen at U.15.c.80.73. Patrol having obtained the information required set off on the return journey. After Patrol had covered 100 yds of the return journey a medium trench mortar burst 100 yards to the right flank. When Patrol had reached a point U.15.c.55.50 another medium trench mortar burst 10 yds on our rear, and Patrol were followed by three more medium T.Ms, all of which however were well in rear. Patrol reached our own lines at 11.35 a.m. & entered the trench at U.20.c.70.80. In addition to the above Patrol observed a track leading from TRIDENT ALLEY U.15.d.80.20 to the sunken road at U.15.c.90.75. The Boche post at U.15.c.80.73 was protected by three pairs of barbed concertinas. (s.) A.F.W. Aickman. Capt. 1/7 (Robin Hood) Bn. Sherwood Foresters.

Sept 28/15.

Patrol Report.

Unit.	Strength of Patrol	Time & Route	Nature of Tasks (Fighting or Reconnaissance &c)	Remarks & Information Route, information gained, action of enemy &c.
9th (Robin Hood) Bn Sherwood Foresters	2 officers (Capt. A. McKechnie & 2/Lt Williamson). 10 O.R. 1 Lewis Gun.	Departure 6 p.m. from U.20.B.70.77. Return 7.25 p.m. to U.20.B.70.77.	To reconnoitre NEPTUNE to ascertain if the enemy held it at night with a Light Machine gun, & post to lie in wait for any enemy patrols between U.21.a.25.60 and U.21.a.30.55.	Patrol left no. 12 post at time & place as stated and proceeded in V shaped formation using NEPTUNE TRENCH as a guide as far as PLUTO PILL BOX. PLUTO was reconnoitred and no signs of enemy when being found patrol advanced towards NEPTUNE PILL BOX. Patrol reached NEPTUNE PILL BOX without encountering the enemy and no signs of enemy occupation whatever were found in NEPTUNE Pill Box. The army being clear, patrol advanced and fired NEPTUNE Pill Box at U.21.a.45.70. at which point patrol lay down & listened. Patrol went up two VEREY Lights from this point but no enemy patrols were seen. After waiting 20 minutes, patrol returned past NEPTUNE pill box & took up a position between U.21.a.25.60 & U.21.a.30.55. & lay in wait for an enemy patrol that might come down the valley or from TRIDENT. Two of the patrol went out to NEPTUNE Pill Box again & fired 8 VEREY lights at intervals to induce the enemy to believe that we held NEPTUNE & to try & draw out one of his patrols. Patrol arrived U.21.a. 7.15 p.m. & the enemy replying to the seven Patrol fired two drums of Lewis down the valley & returned to NEPTUNE. Patrol to U.20.B.70.77. at 7.25 p.m. When patrol had been in our trench 5 minutes the enemy opened fire on NEPTUNE with gas shells.

(S²)

A/Lt W. McKechnie
9th (Robin Hood) Bn
The Sherwood Foresters

Secret   7th Robin Hood Battn. The Sherwoods
                     Defence Scheme   1/1/18
Ref. Map Sheet 51.6.S.W.

1. The Battalion holds in Depth the Right Sub-section of the Left Brigade

2. **Boundaries** On the Right Sunken Road in U.22 —
U.22.a.0.0 – U.21.d.2.9 – PELICAN LANE (Exclusive) – PELICAN AVENUE (inclusive) – U.26.c.1.6 – U.25.d.9.0 – C.1.c.6.0 – B.16.c.9.6
    On the Left U.15.d Central – VULCAN Strong Point (inclusive) – JOVE LANE – QUEENS LANE – STRAY RESERVE (All Exclusive) – U.19.d.9.6 – U.26.a.00.40 – U.25.b.8.1.

3. **Distribution of Troops**   Battalion Headquarters in Railway Reserve at U.25.b.6.2
    Right Front Company Headquarters in VALLEY SUPPORT at U.21.c.4.5.10 with 2 Platoons in Front Line holding Posts Nos. 1, 2, 3, 5, 6, and 2 Platoons in VALLEY SUPPORT. There is an advanced Coy HQ at U.21.c.9.9
    Left Front Company Headquarters in QUEENS LANE at U.20.a.8.5 with 2 Platoons in Front Line holding Posts Nos. 7, 8, 8a, 9, 10, 11, 12 + 2 Platoons in VALLEY SUPPORT
    Support Company in MAN RESERVE with HQ at U.21.c.10.65
    Reserve Company in RAILWAY RESERVE with HQ at U.25.b.8.1

4. **Action in case of attack**   The following are compulsory garrisons in case of attack

Strength	Position	Found by
1 Platoon	MAN RESERVE	Support Coy
3 Platoons	MAN RESERVE Switch and TIGER TRENCH of PELICAN AVENUE	Support Coy

Continued

Sheet 2.

	Action	Strength	Position	Found by
4. Cont'd	in case of Attack	4 Platoons	Trench in front of RAILWAY RESERVE between LEG LANE & PELICAN AVENUE	Reserve Coy

The garrisons of these posts are accomodated in or near their Posts. When there are indications that an enemy attack is imminent, all troops will "STAND TO" and compulsory garrisons will at once man the positions allotted to them.

Should the enemy penetrate into any portion of the front system :—

(1.) Coy concerned will immediately launch a local counter attack with his reserves in VALLEY SUPPORT. He should not fritter away these reserves in small reinforcements

(2.) The Support Coy will launch a counter attack on his own responsibility when he considers the situation demands such action

The launching of this attack will be reported immediately to Battalion H.Q.

(3.) The nearest M.G.s will be informed at once of the locality penetrated.

The reserve Coy will hold the trench in front of RAILWAY RESERVE until relieved by the Support Battn.

On relief it will "STAND TO" in billets & await orders

If tanks are employed by the enemy the Infantry must allow them to pass and leave them to be dealt with by L.G.s & M.G's fire with A.P. bullets and by the Artillery

The S.O.S is to be used only if an enemy attack developes and will only be sent up by Coy commanders or Officer on duty in the front line

Sheet 3

4. Action in case of Attack (contd)

All working Parties working in the Battalion Sector will come under the orders of O/c Battalion

(1). Those working in the Front Line System will occupy the nearest trenches and at once report to nearest Coy HQ

(2). Those working behind the Front Line System will immediately proceed to their "STAND TO" position & report their return to Battn H Qrs

(3). In all cases Officers & NCO's in charge of Working Parties will be prepared to assist in repelling the enemy if necessary.

In the event of the enemy penetrating the defences of the Flank Battalions, action will be as follows –

(1) The Right Front Coy will be prepared to form a defensive flank along PELICAN LANE & PELICAN AVENUE.

(2) The Left Front Coy will be prepared to form a defensive flank along JOVE LANE – QUEENS LANE & LEG LANE

5. Anti-Aircraft Action

Enemy low flying aircraft will be engaged by rifle & L.G. fire, but on no account must enemy aircraft be allowed to direct the attention of the Infantry from an impending attack & no fire which can be brought to bear on advancing Infantry should be directed against aircraft

There will be 1 L.G. for anti-aircraft mounted at Battn H Q & each Coy in the front line will mount one also

6. Administrative Instructions

These have been issued separately

J Fraser
Capt Adjt

7. Acknowledge

Issued at
Distribution – Normal

7th (Robin Hood) Batt The Sherwood Foresters

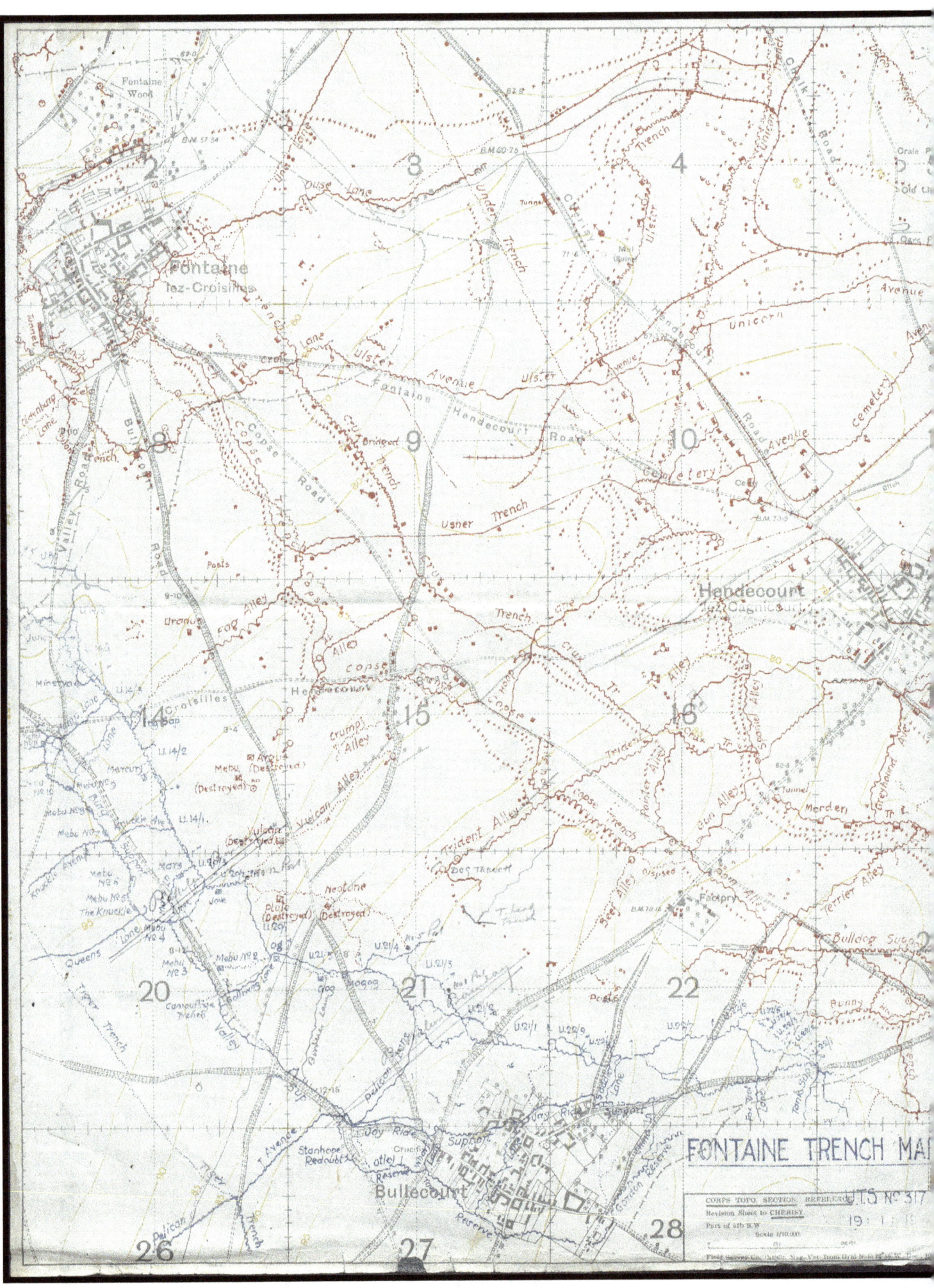

59th Division.
178th Infantry Brigade.

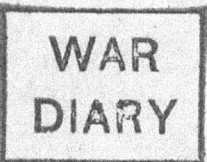

7th BATTALION

SHERWOOD FORESTERS

(Robin Hood Battalion)

MARCH 1918

7th ROBIN HOOD BTN
THE SHERWOOD FORESTERS
MARCH 1st 1918

WAR DIARY
or
INTELLIGENCE SUMMARY
(Erase heading not required.)

Place	Date	Hour	Summary of Events and Information	Remarks and references to Appendices
ECOUST (Left) SECTOR (Brigade) Support	1st		**WORKING PARTY.** A working party consisting of 1 Off + 60 OR worked on TIGER TRENCH from 6.30 PM. to 10.30 PM.	
D.O.	2nd		**Relief.** The Bttn was relieved in the ECOUST (Left) sector by the 22nd Bn the Northumberland Fusiliers. The Bttn moved into Div. Reserve at MORY L'ABBAYE CAMP (B22.A.9.5.) on relief.	AP3 B
MORY L'ABBAYE CAMP. (B22.A.9.5.)	3rd		**Grenades.** Coys were at the disposal of Coy commanders for cadres accompanying the MORY table were allotted the Bn from 10 AM – 6.2 PM. **Working Party.** A working party consisting of 3 Offs + 300 OR. proceeded to NOREUIL on the night 3/4th for the purpose of digging a sunken trench from C.10.b.5.4 to C.5.d.2.2.	

SHEET. No 2.

Army Form C. 2118.

WAR DIARY
or
INTELLIGENCE SUMMARY.

(Erase heading not required.)

Instructions regarding War Diaries and Intelligence Summaries are contained in F. S. Regs., Part II. and the Staff Manual respectively. Title pages will be prepared in manuscript.

Place	Date	Hour	Summary of Events and Information	Remarks and references to Appendices
MORT L'ABBAYE CAMP.	4th		Reveille 6.0 AM. Breakfast 7.0 AM. Sick Parade 7.30 AM. Guard Mounting 5.30 PM. Retreat 6.0 PM. Lights Out 9.15 PM. Staff Parade 9.30 PM. Parade. Coys met at the defence of coy commander for interior economy.	
Do.	5th		Parade. Coys paraded on the football field (B.22.A.6.8) from 9 AM to 1 PM. Having for subject the following: Physical & Bayonet fighting, the new drill musketry. Working Party. A working party consisting of 5 officers & 600 o.r. proceeded to NOREUIL for the purpose of digging communication trench.	
Do.	6th		Parade. The Commanding Officer inspected coys as follows. A. 9 AM B. 10 AM C. 11 AM D.12 noon	

A 5834 Wt. W4973/M687 750,000 8/16 D. D. & L. Ltd. Forms/C.2118/13

SHEET No 3.

Army Form C. 2118.

WAR DIARY
or
INTELLIGENCE SUMMARY.
(Erase heading not required.)

Instructions regarding War Diaries and Intelligence Summaries are contained in F. S. Regs., Part II. and the Staff Manual respectively. Title pages will be prepared in manuscript.

Place	Date	Hour	Summary of Events and Information	Remarks and references to Appendices
MORI L'ABBAYE CAMP.	7th	Parade	Coy paraded on the football field for training from 9AM to 1PM.	
		Court	A Court Martial given to the Pte in the MORS shed by 2/2nd Oxford attended Field Ambulance	
	8th	Parade	Coy paraded from 9AM to 1PM on the football field.	
		Strength Return	LIEUT R.B.KING	
		Duty	LIEUT D.A.MINNICOTT M.C. took over the duties of Intelligence Officer.	
	9th	Parade	Coy paraded for training on the football field for training	

Army Form C. 2118.
SHEET No. 4

WAR DIARY
or
INTELLIGENCE SUMMARY.
(Erase heading not required.)

Place	Date	Hour	Summary of Events and Information	Remarks and references to Appendices
MORY L'ABBAYE CAMP	10th		Parade. The Btn paraded for Divine Service in the theatre MORY at 12 noon	
			Relief. The Btn relieved the 2/6th SOUTH STAFFORDS in the NOREUIL sector on the night 10/11th — Was then in Brigade support with Bttn HQ in sunken road about C9D.9.4.	
Brigade Support. (C9D 9.4.)	11th		Shough Trench. 2/Lieut K.C. Ross killed in action.	
			General. An enemy prisoner was captured on the night 11/12th by the I.S. who took place between the 13th & 15th. The Btn 'stood to' in consequence of	

Army Form C. 2118.

SHEET No 5

WAR DIARY
or
INTELLIGENCE SUMMARY.
(Erase heading not required.)

Instructions regarding War Diaries and Intelligence Summaries are contained in F. S. Regs., Part II. and the Staff Manual respectively. Title pages will be prepared in manuscript.

Place	Date	Hour	Summary of Events and Information	Remarks and references to Appendices
Bryant (Cotes) CAP 94	12th		Situation Very quiet day. Practically no enemy activity	
GRD	13th		Situation At 2am on the morning of the 13th an artillery opened a sharp barrage owing to the S.O.S. being sent from the right front line Btn. The enemy however did not attempt to attack	
GRD	14th		Situation The enemy was still very quiet & no further active bombardments on enemy battery lines were carried out by him. The Btn still continued to "Stand to" from 5.30am to 8.30am	
GRD	15th		Situation Very quiet day & night.	

A5834 Wt.W4973/M687 750,000 8/16 D.D.&L. Ltd. Forms/C.2118/13

WAR DIARY
or
INTELLIGENCE SUMMARY.

(Erase heading not required)

Army Form C. 2118.

SHEET No. 6

Instructions regarding War Diaries and Intelligence Summaries are contained in F. S. Regs., Part II. and the Staff Manual respectively. Title pages will be prepared in manuscript.

Place	Date	Hour	Summary of Events and Information	Remarks and references to Appendices
Brigade Support C9.D.9.b.	16th		**Relief.** The Bn relieved the 2/5 Bn the Sherwood Foresters in the right sector of the Div front on the night 16/17th inst. Relief complete about 3 am. Bn front same as before. Bn H.Q. in shelters near about C.11.C.65.98.	APP D
NOREUIL SECTOR H.Q. (C.15.65.98)	17th		**Situation.** The enemy artillery very quiet & very little movement was seen by our observers.	
	18		**Operations.** At 10.45 pm on the night 18/19th our engineers exploded gas projectors into the enemy line. Observations by our observers from our lines.	
	19th		**Situation.** Very quiet. Our observers report cover is able [?] numbering [?] the enemy lines. Several parties carrying stores [?] observed [?] movement [?] trenches from time to time.	

A7092. W⁺. W12839/M1293 750,000. 1/17. D. D & L¹ Ltd. Forms/C2118/14.

Army Form C. 2118.

Sheet 7

WAR DIARY
or
INTELLIGENCE SUMMARY.
(Erase heading not required.)

Place	Date	Hour	Summary of Events and Information	Remarks and references to Appendices
NOREUIL	20		The day was very quiet. Practically no movement on the enemy's lines was reported by our observers. Weather fine and bright	W.T.
H.Q. at C. 16. c 65.98	21		At 4.56 a.m. the enemy put down a very heavy barrage on the front line systems; trench mortars and field artillery continued the bombardment at an intense rate until about 7.45 a.m. At the same time, our battery positions were heavily engaged by the enemy's heavy and field artillery. At 5.5 a.m. communication by wire to Btts. H.Q. was broken & the only message that went through after that was one by pigeon timed 6 a.m. reporting a heavy bombardment. At about 8 a.m. the shelling, which had been very lengthy good, changed to H.E. At about 10 a.m. the barrage was reported to have lifted on to the second system, i.e. it was behind the Battalion. Only 14 men escaped unwounded from the Battalion and it appears from their reports that the enemy broke through on both flanks, and coming behind the QUEANT - ECOUST railway cut off and very likely surrounded the Battalion. This must have been	

Sheet 8

Army Form C. 2118.

WAR DIARY
or
INTELLIGENCE SUMMARY.
(Erase heading not required.)

Place	Date	Hour	Summary of Events and Information	Remarks and references to Appendices
		between 9-30 and 10 a.m. Captain H.C. WRIGHT and Lieut. G.W. BLOODWORTH were wounded and escaped; all the other officers are still missing, with the exception of 2/Lieut. J.L. MOY and 2/Lieut. A.G.F. MELHUISH who were reported killed. Owing to this and to the capture of all documents at Battalion Headquarters, no accurate or detailed account of the action is possible. During the evening as far men who were not in the forward line of the Reserve line of Third System Support line of the Third system were taken up to man the Third System, the of the Third system soon taken over by the 177th Infantry Brigade, who had been acting as the firing line of the Third system by the 40th Division. Casualties and appreciations by the Coys and Brigade Commanders are attached in the Appendices.				W.F.
22			The remaining men of the Battalion who had not been in the line were collected and sent up to the Reserve line 3rd System, on the right of MORY with details from the rest of the Brigade	W.F.

SHEET 1. No. 9

Army Form C. 2118.

WAR DIARY
or
INTELLIGENCE SUMMARY.
(Erase heading not required.)

Place	Date	Hour	Summary of Events and Information	Remarks and references to Appendices
3rd Defence line B.25.3.6.	22nd		Situation: 45 ORs were collected, consisting of men returned from leave & convalescents & sent up to reinforce the 2nd Defence line under Capt SPATCHER.	
	23rd		The transport moved back to COURCELLES in the early morning of the 23rd, waggon teams parked on ground to the west of the village, it was again ordered to move to ground west of the ABLAINZEVILLE — AYETTE Rd. Situation.	
	24th		The event under Capt QUIBELL took out a position on the high ground about B.25.2.8. & were not attacked again.	
	25th		The transport moved to SENLIS on the night 24th & were ground at this place by 2/Lieut Spatcher & 37 ORs. On the night 25/26th the Bun moved from SENLIS to BAVINCOURT	
	26TH		The Bun remained at BAVINCOURT during the 26th & moved to	

SHEET. No 10

Army Form C. 2118.

WAR DIARY
or
INTELLIGENCE SUMMARY.
(Erase heading not required.)

Place	Date	Hour	Summary of Events and Information	Remarks and references to Appendices
BAVINCOURT	26th		FIEFFES on the 27th	
	27th		FIEFFES The Bn remained at FIEFFES during the 27-28th & moved by train from CANDAS to LAPUGNOY & thence to HERMIN by motor bus on the night 28/29th arriving early on the morning of the 29.	
	29th		HERMIN The Bn remained at HERMIN during the 29th, 30th & 31st & was visited by the Majesty the King on the 30st.	
			General The total casualties to the Bn amounted to 26 officers & 629 OR.	

A R.B. Kirchen — Major
Comdg 7th (Robin Hood) BATTn. (SHERWOOD FORESTERS, NOTTS. & DERBY REGT.)

APPENDIX 'A'.

			Officers.	O.Ranks.
Total strength of Battalion Mar.1. 1918.			50.	1040.
Total Fighting Strength	36.	834.		
On Command.				
Bde & Div. Employ.	2.	55.		
T.M.Battery.		9.		
Leave.	4.	25.		
Hospital.		26.		
Courses.	7.	42.		
Depot Battalion.	1.	34.		
2 Coy.A.S.C.		2.		
170 Tun. Coy.R.E.		13.		
	50.	1040.	50.	1040.
Total Strength March 1.1918.			50.	1040.
Increase.				
Reinforcements		31.		
Rejoined.	1.	17.	1.	48.
			51.	1088.
Decrease.				
Missing.	23.	614.		
Killed.	1.	2.		
Wounded.	3.	18.		
Died of Wounds.		2.		
Evacuated.		76.		
England.(Tour of Home duty).	2.			
England Sick.	1.			
Base.	1.			
Surplus Per.	1.	5.		
Employment Base.		2.		
England Comm.		2.		
To. M.G. Coy.		4.	32.	725.
	32.	725.	19.	363.
Total strength of Battalion Mar.31st 1918.			19.	363.
Total Fighting Strength	12.	189.		
On Command.				
On Detachment.	7.	174.		
	19.	363.	19.	363.

APPENDIX 'A'

45th I.B. 7/5/17   Copy
470 Fd A Coy RE
178 Fd A

  I would like to have been the first to tell the Brigade personally how much I appreciated their effort on 21st & 22nd March, but now that His Majesty the King and the G.O.C. Division have both inspected the Brigade and talked to them, I feel I cannot possibly add anything to what they have said in the way of praising their high fighting qualities.

  It might be of interest to all to know that all my telephone lines to the 3 Battalions in the line were broken during the first 10 minutes of the bombardment, and beyond talking to the Signalling Officer of 2/6th Battalion Lieut. HICKMAN, about 5.5 am I had no communication whatever with them except as follows:-

  A wireless message came in from 1st Battalion to say that their right and left front companies reported they were being heavily bombarded at 6.30 am. A message by pigeon was sent off at 10.30 am by 2/6 Bn to say the enemy had

2

broken through on both their flanks but they were still holding out. Three or four messages by runner were received from 2/5th Bn; the last one was timed 12 noon saying that Colonel GADD and 150 men were holding out in the Sunken Road between NOREUIL and LONGATTE and that the enemy had taken DEWSBURY and PONTEFRACT trenches and was working round his right.

There is no doubt that the Brigade delayed the enemy's attack long enough for reinforcements to be brought up — to stop it altogether would have been impossible.

It took the enemy 4 hours to advance 2,500 yards.

There were undoubtedly 4 Divisions if not 5, against us.

I only wish to add that I am prouder than ever of the Brigade & that I deeply regret the heavy losses incurred to all those gallant officers & men who are killed, wounded or missing.

(Sd) T.W. STANSFELD Brig-Genl
Commdg 178 Inf Bde

30.3.18

		1750/16.G.
176th Inf.Bdo.	59th Bn.M.G.C.	30.3.18.
177th " "	6/7th R.Scots Fusrs.	
178th " "	Div.Train.	
C.R.A.	A.D.M.S.	
C.R.E.	D.A.D.V.S.	
Signals.	D.A.D.O.S.	

****

The following extract from a letter addressed to the Divisional Commander by Lieutenant-General Sir J. Aylmer Haldane, K.C.B., D.S.O., Commanding VI Corps is published for information.

R. G. Gorton
Bt.Colonel,
G.S. 59th Division.

30.3.18.

Will you please convey to all ranks of your Division my admiration and thanks for the very gallant stand they made against overwhelming numbers of the enemy supported by a tremendous artillery.

The Division nobly did their duty on the right of VI Corps, and from all accounts that have reached me have inflicted heavy loss upon the enemy. I grieve for the heavy casualties among your gallant officers N.C.Os and men, but the 59th Division have the satisfaction of knowing that they did their duty in as trying circumstances as can possibly happen in war.

178th Brigade.

59th Division.

1/7th BATTALION

NOTTS & DERBY REGIMENT

APRIL 1918.

Army Form C. 2118.

WAR DIARY
or
INTELLIGENCE SUMMARY.

(Erase heading not required.)

7th (Res...) Division Header — April 1918
Ref. Map FRANCE & BELGIUM
Sheets 27 and 28

Place	Date	Hour	Summary of Events and Information	Remarks and references to Appendices
PROVEN	1/4/18		The Battalion arrived PROVEN by train from AUBIGNY, marched to the Battalion lines at KINDERHOEK, arrived 3 am into huts.	
"	2/4/18	9 am	Staff of 4/6 N.C.O.'s officers arrived & were distributed amongst companies	
"	3/4/18	3 pm	General Plumer, commanding 2nd Army inspected the 178 Bde & addressed the officers	
WINNIZEELE	14/4/18	11 am	Batt. moved to WINNIZEELE. Orders received ... from No 2 ...	
BRANDOCK	14/4/18	4 pm	Batt. moved by train to POPERINGHE and marched to TOKIO camp, BRANDHOEK	
KEMMEL	12/4/18	12 am	Batt. received immediate orders to entrain at BRANDHOEK. It entrained at La CLYTIE and marched to cross roads N.26.b.91 after moving from the Batt bivouacked in camp at N.1.6.6 ... during the night. Orders were received to move at once towards NEUVE EGLISE to attack up the saturion there	
NEUVE EGLISE	13/4/18		The Battn. pushed forward the Battn. acting as a guard as far as LINDEN. This was done. Later consisting of the 8th King section moved forward by ? & the Bttn ... NEUVE ... Remainder of Bgn with Bn H.Q. ?/46 L.I.+5 ... the ..... had ? ... ? ...	
NEUVE EGLISE			NEUVE EGLISE held in situation ... ... though a know that the situation ... Battn. H.Q. at ...	

Army Form C. 2118.

4th (Reserve Bn?) Sherwood Foresters - April

WAR DIARY
or
INTELLIGENCE SUMMARY.
(Erase heading not required.)

Instructions regarding War Diaries and Intelligence Summaries are contained in F. S. Regs., Part II. and the Staff Manual respectively. Title pages will be prepared in manuscript.

Place	Date	Hour	Summary of Events and Information	Remarks and references to Appendices
WULVERGHEM	14/4/18	1 am	Batln relieved the 13th R.I.R. and took up front line positions. A+B Coys were on the front line from NIEULANDFARM Tne.7 along road to T6.d.3.2 thence to T.11.a.8.5 BHQ was at T.11.c.2.8. Troops on the right were reported to have withdrawn so that support & reserve Coys moved up to fill the gap. "B" Coy were attacked, but the enemy were easily repulsed.	
KEMMEL	15/4/18		New line taken up approximately from DAYLIGHT CORNER to LINDENHOEK. BHQ was in MONT KEMMEL N.26.c.	
"	16/4/18 2 am		Line withdrawn and Batln moved into Bde reserve with BHQ at N.25.b.9.1. Coys extending along LINDENHOEK CROSS ROADS – KEMMEL – thence along LOCRE roads – Centrals pts were at N.21.d.4.b – link trade N.26.c.9.1 & 9.6 & trans trade N.19.c.8.0 – B.L Reserve Coy was N.25.b.	
"	16/4/18 9 pm		Batln relieved 2/6 S.F. who side-stepped to the right. That BHQ remained if N.25.b.9.1 while 2nd BHQ moved to 2/6 S.F. BHQ. The Northern front ran through N.27.c. to N.32.b.5.1.	
"	19/4/18 10 am		Enemy attacking front line by Batts. He was driven off. Shelling by Arty & Bdes with H.E.s & gas shells continued throughout the day, but guidedual considerably by dusk when the attack was at not from the LINDENHOEK – NEUVE EGLISE road. No enemy were seen in front nor indeed is there.	

7th (Robin Hoods) Sherwood Foresters - April

WAR DIARY
or
INTELLIGENCE SUMMARY.
(Erase heading not required.)

Army Form C. 2118.

Instructions regarding War Diaries and Intelligence Summaries are contained in F. S. Regs., Part II. and the Staff Manual respectively. Title pages will be prepared in manuscript.

Place	Date	Hour	Summary of Events and Information	Remarks and references to Appendices
KEMMEL	18/4/18		Enemy a few shelled heavily with HE's & gas all day, but no attack developed	
			Patrol an gas left our lines at dusk along the road previously investigated but observed nothing	
	19/4/18		The shelling was comparatively light during the day, but from HQ a very heavy bombardment about 4 pm after enemy air craft had been over our lines	
	19/4/18	12 midnight	The Battn was relieved by the 4 mod A, 6 C. P. bats were taken over by the 9 B Company of Regiment Leinster Regt, 2 safe half about the 2/1 S.E. the night previous and B C.P. bats were taken over by the 2/6 S. Staff Regiment we had relieved the R.I.R. on C Company on by the 3/D C.P. were there with others. The Battn then marched to & encamped at WESTOUTRE	
BRANDHOEK	20/4/18	10am	Battn entrained at WESTOUTRE for VLAMERTINGHE encamped in huts for one night in the wood at	
HOUTKERQUE	21/4/18 11:30am		Battn marched to HOUTKERQUE were & encamped in huts just outside village. Here the Battn received reinforcements and commenced re-organising & training in readiness for future operations	
	23/4/18 12 noon		Brig. Gen Stansfeld of the 148 Inf Bde congratulated the Officers & the Battn specially in its fine work	

Army Form C. 2118.

7th (Robin Hood) Sherwood Foresters - April

WAR DIARY
or
INTELLIGENCE SUMMARY.
(Erase heading not required.)

Place	Date	Hour	Summary of Events and Information	Remarks and references to Appendices
PROVEN	26/4/18	5.30pm	Immediate orders received at 3.45pm to be ready to move at short notice. The Battn orders received at 5.00pm. Fighting orders to ROAD CAMP, PROVEN. (F25d, sh. 27)	
"	27/4/18	9am	Battn ready to move into action if required at shortest notice. At 10am orders were received to carry on the usual training.	
	28/4/18	10am	The Commanding Officer reconnoitred the "Army Line", with special reference to the portion occupied by the 59th Div; the 177 & 176 Inf. Bdes were already in position while the 118 was in Reserve. At 10pm orders were received to move, on the following days, back to the HOUTKERQUE area.	
HOUTKERQUE	29/4/18	6.30am	Battn marched back & took over their old camp near HOUTKERQUE village.	

W. Foster Capt & Adjt.

[signature] O.C. 7th (Robin Hood) BATTn. (SHERWOOD FORESTERS.) (NOTTS. & DERBY REGT.)

30TH DIVISION
21st Infy Bde

7TH BN SHERWOOD FOR.
MAY 1918

7th Sherwoods

To 39 DIV

Confidential

Vol. 16

21/30 W.O.T. P. Wink.

WAR DIARY
of the
7th SHERWOOD Foresters
For the
Month of MAY. 1918.

WAR DIARY 7th (Robin Hoods) Sherwood Foresters
INTELLIGENCE SUMMARY

May 1918

Army Form C. 2118.

Place	Date	Hour	Summary of Events and Information	Remarks and references to Appendices
HOUTKERQUE	1.5.18	9am	Usual training program	
"	2.5.18	8.30am	All tents struck preparatory to Battn marching to KIYa 2 & WATOU area. 'B' Coy moved off at 9.30am as Advanced Party and erected the tents in new area. Remainder of Battn moved off at 2.30pm	W.F
WATOU AREA KIYa 2.8	3.5.18	9am	Usual parades up to 11.30am. At 12.30pm Battn proceeded to the WATOU-ABEELE switch line and dug trenches	W.F.
"	4.5.18	9am	Parades & digging as above	
"	5.5.18	8am	Immediate orders received for Battn to move to STOMER Battn marched off at 8.30am	W.F.
"	"		& WATOU & proceeded by bus to CASERNE DELABARRE barracks.	
STOMER	6.5.18	8.30pm	Information to hand that the 1st Battn S.F. is to be reduced in establishment to a Training Cadre W.F. consisting roughly of 1 Battn HQ & Coy HQ, as a temporary measure, owing to a shortage of reinforcements. Brigadier Genl. Stanfield addressed the Battn, complimented it on its splendid record and informed his troops that such reductions was necessary	W.F.
"	7.5.18	2.15	Major-Genl. Bremen addressed the Battn in similar terms to the Brig: General, remarking that the Robin Hoods formed one of his best battalions Battn less Training Cadre & TRANSPORT marched to WATTEN & entrained for CALAIS. 22 Officers and 620 O.R. were transferred to "R" Infantry Base Depot	W.F
"	8.5.18	9am	Stores handed out to ORDNANCE.	

WAR DIARY
INTELLIGENCE SUMMARY

Army Form C. 2118.

7th (Robin Hoods) Sherwood Foresters

May 1918

Place	Date	Hour	Summary of Events and Information	Remarks and references to Appendices
BLESSY	9.5.18	8 am	Battn. Training Staff and TRANSPORT, (13 officers, the Interpreter, and 100 other ranks) marched to BLESSY.	W.F
BOURS	10.5.18	8.15 am	Battn. marched to BOURS. Bde H.Q. was at GRICOURT and after 13th at DIEVAL	W.F
"	15.5.18	1 pm	The Transport left the Battn. for ETAPLES. (one G.S. wagon, one Officers Mess Cart, one Water-Cart, and 12 horses were left with the Battn. The Signalling officers, Lewis Gun Officer and Scout officer were each allowed a bicycle.	W.F
			20, N.yorks. Battn. gave C.O. Commander reconnoitred new defensive systems the 'B.B.' Line.	W.F
	16.5.18	4.30	Three C.O. Commanders proceeded to DIEVAL and went by Lorry to be attached to the R.E.s to assist in superintending the laying out and digging a part of the new line.	W.F
	19.5.18	2 pm	The Quartermaster proceeded to the 2nd Garrison Battn. Royal Irish Rifles, who were also assisting in digging, to give advice as regards the method of procedure adopted in this country. N.C.Os also proceeded at various dates for the same purpose.	W.F

WAR DIARY 7th (Robin Hood) Sherwood Foresters

INTELLIGENCE SUMMARY.

May 1918

Place	Date	Hour	Summary of Events and Information	Remarks and references to Appendices
BOURS	27/5/18	5 pm	Orders received for the recall of the Company Commanders & the Quartermasters to units.	W.F
	28/5/18	3 pm	Entrained at PERNES en route for ABBEVILLE	W.F
	29/5/18	7 am	Arrived at ABBEVILLE. Here the Battn were met by a Guide sent by the 21st Brigade. The Guide conducted the Battn to CAUMONT. The Battn now attached to the 21st Bde of the 30th Div; for the purpose of training Americans	W.F
	30/5/18	10 am	Brig: Gen: 21st Bde visited BHQ and outlined generally the method of training to be adopted.	W.F

R.B. Brickman Lieut Colonel
Comdg 7th (Robin Hood) BATTn.
(SHERWOOD FORESTERS,)
(NOTTS. & DERBY REGT.)

Army Form C. 2118.

WAR DIARY
or
INTELLIGENCE SUMMARY.
(Erase heading not required.)

Instructions regarding War Diaries and Intelligence Summaries are contained in F.S. Regs., Part II. and the Staff Manual respectively. Title pages will be prepared in manuscript.

Place	Date	Hour	Summary of Events and Information	Remarks and references to Appendices
CAUMONT	1-3 JUNE	—	The battalion training staff remained at CAUMONT pending the arrival of the 30th American division in this area.	N/2
do	4	—	The 131st American I.R. detrained at OISEMONT and billeted in the CAUMONT area. Being affiliated for training to 9th Sherwood Foresters training staff	N/2
FRUCOURT	5	—	Battalion H.Q. and "D" Coy cadre moved with 131st American Regimental H.Q to FRUCOURT. "A" Coy detached to 2nd battn 131. I.R. at HOCQUINCOURT "B" - - 1st - - CITERNE "C" - - 3rd - - FRUCOURT.	N/2
do	6-9.	—	The training staffs assisted the Americans in training and organisation as detailed by the 4.O.C. 2.13th I.B. (British)	N/2
do	10	—	131st I.R. left CAUMONT-FRUCOURT area. The Battalion training cadre concentrated in FRUCOURT.	N/2
do	11	—	Remained in FRUCOURT area training.	N/2

Army Form C. 2118.

WAR DIARY
or
INTELLIGENCE SUMMARY.
(Erase heading not required.)

Instructions regarding War Diaries and Intelligence Summaries are contained in F.S. Regs., Part II. and the Staff Manual respectively. Title pages will be prepared in manuscript.

Place	Date	Hour	Summary of Events and Information	Remarks and references to Appendices
MONCHAUX	12	JUNE	Under orders from 21st I.B. (British) the battalion training cadre route marched to MONCHAUX and billeted there.	W
do.	13-14	—	The training cadre remained in the MONCHAUX area. Tactical schemes of an offensive nature for officers & N.C.O's were practised.	W
MONCHY-SUR-EU	15	—	The training cadre was transferred to the 198th J.B. (British), and proceeded by route march to MONCHY-SUR-EU, for affiliation to 2nd Battn. 131.I.R. Company cadres were attached to the corresponding American companies.	W
do.	16-20	—	Remained at MONCHY-SUR-EU. Training carried out for six hours daily, in accordance with the American Schedule. It included musketry, gas, Lewis gun instruction, and the mechanism of the Lee-Enfield rifle. American and British transport proceeded by three days march work to PIERREGOT.	W
do.	20	—	The training cadre accompanied 2nd Battn. 131.I.R. by bus route to PIERREGOT, where both were accommodated under canvas. The three battns.	W
PIERREGOT	21	—	and H.Q. of the 131.I.R. were concentrated in the village. Battn H.Q. and "C" Coy training cadres were re-affiliated to American Regimental H.Q. 131.I.R.	W

A 5834   Wt. W4973/M687   750,000   8/16   D. D. & L. Ltd.   Forms/C.2118/13

Army Form C. 2118.

WAR DIARY
or
INTELLIGENCE SUMMARY.
(Erase heading not required.)

Instructions regarding War Diaries and Intelligence Summaries are contained in F. S. Regs., Part II. and the Staff Manual respectively. Title pages will be prepared in manuscript.

Place	Date	Hour	Summary of Events and Information	Remarks and references to Appendices
PIERREGOT	22 JUNE	—	American and British transport marched in. Battalion & coy commanders of American units reconnoitred VADEN LINE.	1/10
CONTAY	23-24	—	13/1 I.R. occupied the VADEN LINE [CONTAY SECTOR] for twenty four hours, for practice purposes. Returned to PIERREGOT on the evening of the 24th inst.	1/10
PIERREGOT	25-26	—	Training continued according to schedule. Special instruction in Lewis gunnery, range practices, and night digging.	1/10
ST. LEGER-LE-DOMART	27	—	Under orders from 66th Div (British) Battalion training cadre moved by march route to the ST. LEGER staging area, and billeted the night in the town.	1/10
VILLERS-SOUS-AILLY	28	—	Training cadre was transferred to 199 I.B. (British) and proceeded by march route to VILLERS-SOUS-AILLY, being attached on arrival to 2/5 Batt. 130 I.R.	1/10
do	29-30	—	Training continued according to American schedules including Gas, musketry, Bombing and Range practices. An epidemic influenza made its appearance on the 29th inst, infecting all officers except the C.O. and much handicapping the progress of training.	1/10

R.B. McKinnon Lieut. Col.
7th (Robin Hood) Battn. (NOTTS. & DERBY REGT.)
Commdg

7th. (Robin Hood) Battalion, The Sherwood Foresters.

APPENDIX 'A'.

Strength of Training Cadre on 31st. May 1918.   10.   59.

    Training Cadre.   10.   49.
    On leave.   2.
    Courses.   1.
    59th. Div. Sig. Coy.   2.
    178th. Bde. Employ.   4.
    Gun Park WATTEN.   1.
                        10.   59.   10.   59.

Strength of Training Cadre 1st. June. 1918.   10.   59.

    Increase.
      Reinforcements.   5.   5.
    Decrease.   10.   64.
      Absorbed into 178
      Bde. H.Q.   3.
      Trans. to 59 Div. Sig. Coy.   1.
      To Base Depot.   5.   9.
                                           10.   55.

Strength of Training Cadre 1st. July 1918.   10.   55.

CONFIDENTIAL.

WAR DIARY.
- OF -
7TH. (ROBIN HOOD) BN. THE SHERWOOD FORESTERS.

FROM - 1st. July, 1918.
TO - 31st. July, 1918.

VOLUME 42.

7th (Robin Hood) Battalion
The Sherwood Foresters

Army Form C. 2118.

WAR DIARY
or
INTELLIGENCE SUMMARY.
(Erase heading not required.)

July 1918

Instructions regarding War Diaries and Intelligence Summaries are contained in F.S. Regs., Part II. and the Staff Manual respectively. Title pages will be prepared in manuscript.

Place	Date	Hour	Summary of Events and Information	Remarks and references to Appendices
VILLERS-SOUS-AILLY (Sheet 11, A6)	2/7/18		The Battalion Training Cadre was in billets at VILLERS-SOUS-AILLY, supervising the training of the 2nd Battn. 130th Infantry Regiment A.E.F. The tactical training carried out was entirely of an offensive nature, consisting chiefly of company and platoon attacks, advanced guards, and patrolling. Many of these practices were carried out with both ammunition and assisted co-operation of Vickers and Lewis Machine Guns. Other units continuously in training, musketry, Lewis Gunnery and Bayonet fighting.	W.F.
	4th		A detachment consisting of "B" and "C" Coys, under Captain W. MULLIGAN was sent to MONFLIERES (Attrieville 14, K5) to supervise the training of the 3rd Battalion 130th Inf. Regt. A.E.F. This training was carried out on the same lines as for the 2nd Battn. (above). Both battalions were keen and of fine physique, and were ready to take	W.F.

WAR DIARY
or
INTELLIGENCE SUMMARY.
(Erase heading not required.)

Army Form C. 2118.

Place	Date	Hour	Summary of Events and Information	Remarks and references to Appendices
	15th		Part in any operations. The American battalions left the area, and the detachment at MONFLIERES returned to VILLERS.	B.T
	21st to 31st		The Battalion Training Staff entrained at PONT-REMY and moved by rail to ABANCOURT (Dieppe 16, J4) where they went under canvas. On arrival the Battalion came under the 198th Inf. Brigade.	
ABANCOURT			While at ABANCOURT, Training was carried out during the mornings within the Cadre in Lewis Gunnery, Musketry and Gas. In addition, Lewis Gun, Musketry and Bombing Instructors were supplied to the Battalions of the 198th Inf. Brigade.	N.T.
	22nd		Captain W. MULLIGAN posted to 1st Bn. Wiltshire Regt. and struck off strength.	

R.B. Pickman Lieut-Colonel
Coty. 7th (Robin Hood) Battn. (SHERWOOD FORESTERS.
NOTTS. & DERBY REGT)

1/8/18

APPENDIX 'A'.

Strength of Training Cadre 1-7-18.

	Officers.	O. Ranks.
Training Cadre.	8.	46.
Leave.	1.	2.
Courses.	1.	3.
59th. Divl. Emp.		1.
178 Bde. Employ.		1.
	__10.__	__53.__

Total Strength July 1st. 1918.   10.   53.

Increase. Nil.

Decrease.
Trans. to 1st. Wilts.	1.	—
Trans to 59th.Divl. Sig. Coy.	—	1.
Trans to 178 T.M.B.	—	1.
To Base Depot.	—	1.
	__1.__	__3.__
	__9.__	__50.__

Strength July 31st. 1918.
Training Cadre.	7.	47.
Leave.	2.	2.
Attd. 1st. Wilts.		1.
H.Q. Abancourt Area.		1.
Signal Sch. III Corps.		—
	__9.__	__50.__
	__9.__	__50.__

Appendix "B"

Honours and Awards, announced during July 1918.

Army Form W. 3121.

Schedule No.	Unit	Regtl. No.	Rank and Name	Action for which commended	Recommended by	Honour or Reward	(To be left blank)
	7th Sherwood Foresters	265188	Serjeant (now C.S.M) HARRISON, THOMAS FREDERICK	At NEUVE EGLISE and LINDENHOEK on April 13th and 18th, respectively, this N.C.O. carried out difficult and dangerous patrols, securing much information of great value.	Lt-Colonel R.B. RICKMAN	MILITARY MEDAL (Immediate) Awarded	
	"	265100	Lance-Serjeant (now Serjeant) BURTON, JAMES HENRY.	In the operations near MOUNT KEMMEL between April 13th and 19th, this N.C.O. showed remarkable bravery on several occasions. In the front line under the worst possible conditions, he was always cool and cheerful, and kept the morale of his platoon up to a high standard.	"	MILITARY MEDAL (Immediate) Awarded	

www.ingramcontent.com/pod-product-compliance
Lightning Source LLC
Chambersburg PA
CBHW081450160426
43193CB00013B/2428